Biblical Meditation

Biblical Truth Simply Explained

Biblical Meditation

Campbell McAlpine

Chosen Books
A Division of Baker Book House Co
Grand Rapids, Michigan 49516

Published in the USA in 2004 by Chosen Books
a division of Baker Book House Company
P.O. Box 6287, Grand Rapids, MI 49516-6287
www.bakerbooks.com

Originally published under the title *Explaining Biblical Meditation* by Sovereign
World Limited of Tonbridge, Kent, England

Printed in the United States of America

Library of Congress Cataloging-in-Publication Data
McAlpine, Campbell.
   Biblical meditation / Campbell McAlpine.
     p. cm. — (Biblical truth simply explained)
   Originally published: Tonbridge, Kent, England : Sovereign World, 1991.
   ISBN 0-8007-9371-4 (pbk.)
   1. Meditation—Biblical teaching. I. Title. II. Series.

BS680.M38M23 2004
248.3′4—dc22

2003062620

Notes for Study Leaders

This book is a practical study of biblical meditation. The teaching is not just meant to be discussed—it is to be responded to. Five study questions at the end of each chapter are designed to help members of a study group both to think about and engage personally with this subject.

As a leader you will need to balance the needs of individuals with those of the whole group. Do not be surprised if different opinions and feelings arise during the study, particularly when people answer certain questions. It is wise not to get sidetracked into devoting too much time to any one person's thoughts, but to enable everyone in the group to share and respond to the positive message of the book.

Encourage group members to read one chapter prior to each meeting and to think about the issues in advance. Review the content of the chapter at the meeting to refresh everyone's memory and avoid embarrassing those who have not managed to do the "homework." If the study takes place in a receptive, encouraging atmosphere, it will help members to share.

Pray together and ask for God's assistance, which will help you all to take hold of the truths presented. Our hope is that as readers explore this vital theme of biblical meditation, they will experience increasing fruitfulness in their lives.

May God bless you as you study this material yourself and lead others in doing so.

Contents

Foreword

As you read this book and apply its truths, I believe it will revolutionize your life. This is not a human assertion or exaggeration but a God-given promise to everyone who meditates day and night on His Word:

> He is like a tree planted by streams of water,
>   which yields its fruit in season
> and whose leaf does not wither.
> Whatever he does prospers.
>
> Psalm 1:3

The most important words written in this book are Scriptures. I encourage the reader to read each one carefully and prayerfully, because light comes through God's Word.

I am indebted to all who have influenced my life to love God and to love His Word: To my parents, whose address is heaven; to my wife, Shelagh, my constant encourager; to many wonderful friends; and to all whose ministry or writing has enhanced my knowledge of our God and Savior, Jesus Christ. Greatest thanks of all to Him who is the Word of Life, who loved me and gave Himself for me.

1

The Importance of Meditation

The subject of this minibook is biblical meditation, which is probably the most neglected of all devotional practices and yet the most profitable. No earthly wealth could purchase its benefits, because the Word of God "is more precious to me than thousands of pieces of silver and gold" (Psalm 119:72). The knowledge of God's Word is the greatest need of those who claim to have a relationship with Him.

We are in the time predicted by Isaiah the prophet:

> See, darkness covers the earth
>   and thick darkness is over the peoples,
> but the LORD rises upon you
>   and his glory appears over you.
>
> Isaiah 60:2

The Church of the living God has to stand, that the power of the Almighty might be manifested through her. She must stand upright, so that she might be the light in the darkness that God intended her to be.

Daniel reminded us that "the people who know their God will firmly resist him [the enemy]. Those who are wise will instruct many" (Daniel 11:32–33). As never before, it is essential for all Christians to examine their attitude to God's Word and the way they are developing their knowledge of it.

At great price the treasures of the Bible have been given to us over the centuries, and no one has an excuse for ignorance. The knowledge of God is available to all who will give their heart and time to its pursuit. It is the desire of His great heart that we might go on to know Him and be effective in these last days.

Paul encouraged the church at Corinth with these words: "For God, who said, 'Let light shine out of darkness,' made his light shine in our hearts to give us the light of the knowledge of the glory of God in the face of Christ" (2 Corinthians 4:6). The light of the glorious Gospel has already shone in our hearts, but we can continually receive more light and more treasure through knowing the Lord better.

Have you ever wondered why David knew God so well? He wrote most of the largest book of the Bible, the Psalms. More of David's prayers and more of his worship are recorded than those of anyone else. Yet David did not possess much of the written word; he did not study at a Bible school or theological college; he did not have a church to go to; he did not have a library full of commentaries or even recordings of wonderful preachers. What was the key to his knowledge and insight? One answer is that he *meditated*.

When Joshua took over from Moses the awesome task of leading the children of Israel, he had reason to be scared to death. Would you not have been? However, God spoke to him with encouragement and instruction:

> Be strong and courageous, because you will lead these people to inherit the land I swore to their forefathers to give them. Be strong and very courageous. Be careful to obey all the law my servant Moses gave you; do not turn from it to the right or to the left, that you may be successful wherever you go. Do not let this Book of the Law depart from your mouth; meditate on it day and night, so that you may be careful to do everything written in it. Then you will be prosperous and successful.
>
> Joshua 1:6–8

God gave Joshua a key: to meditate.

Paul, writing to Timothy, also encouraged him to "Be diligent in these matters; give yourself wholly to them, so that everyone may see your progress" (1 Timothy 4:15). The King James Version translates the words "Be diligent in these matters" as "Meditate upon these things."

Whenever there is the real, there is also the counterfeit. One deceit that has ensnared millions is TM, or "Transcendental Meditation." Its partly humanistic and partly Eastern religious philosophy declares that the answers to human questions and questing are within us. It asserts that those practicing TM can arrive at a mental state called "pure being" or "bliss consciousness," free from thought or symbol.

We have been created to meditate upon God, His character, His words, His works and His ways. The mantra repeated in TM cannot replace revelation by the Holy Spirit. It fails to acknowledge or deal with the greatest human problem, sin, and therefore eliminates the need for God's answer—a Savior, Jesus Christ the Lord.

Thank God, we can say no to the counterfeit, and yes to what is real and authentic. Biblical meditation will revolutionize our lives when it becomes a continual part of our devotion and a consistent feature of our life. Despite the words and images of the world swirling around, meditation can transform the way we think and speak.

Then we can join the psalmist in his cry:

> May the words of my mouth and the meditation of my heart
>   be pleasing in your sight,
> O Lord, my Rock and my Redeemer.

Psalm 19:14

Prayer

Father, I come to You in the name of the Lord Jesus. I desire to know You better through Your Word. By Your Holy Spirit I want to be equipped to know You and do Your will in these perilous times. Please teach me how to meditate on Your Scriptures and make them an integral part of my life. I trust You to do this. Amen.

Study questions:

1. What is the importance of really knowing God's Word?
2. How have you previously viewed meditation?
3. What do we see in the Bible about the practice of scriptural meditation?
4. How do we know Transcendental Meditation is a counterfeit?
5. Do you want to know God better?

2

The Companions of Meditation

When considering a truth from God's Word, it is important to ensure that it is interwoven with other truth. Although biblical meditation is one of the most rewarding means of obtaining heart knowledge of God, the other means must never be neglected.

Let us briefly consider the other ways.

Hearing God's Word

Knowledge is impossible without communication, and God has chosen different ways by which He makes Himself known. One of these ways is listening to Scripture as it is read and hearing what God is saying. However, many times in church, instead of intently listening to the Bible reading, we wait to hear what the preacher is going to say about it.

Two words are frequently used in Scripture, "hear" and "listen." We can hear multitudes of words, and they can be just meaningless sound to us. However, when we listen, or "hearken" as the King James Version translates it, we give our full attention. We listen carefully because we believe that what we are hearing is of great value. It is the very Word of God.

The message to all the churches in Asia was, "He who has an ear, let him hear what the Spirit says to the churches" (Revelation 2:7).

Amos prophesied:

> "The days are coming," declares the Sovereign Lord,
>   "when I will send a famine through the land—
> not a famine of food or a thirst for water,
>   but a famine of hearing the words of the Lord.
> Men will stagger from sea to sea
>   and wander from north to east,
> searching for the word of the Lord,
>   but they will not find it."

Amos 8:11–12

Notice that Amos did not say there would be a famine of preaching, or conferences, or church services, but of properly hearing the Word of God. In Scripture, hearing is linked with obeying, believing and receiving God's words. "Do not merely listen to the word, and so deceive yourselves. Do what it says" (James 1:22).

Reading God's Word

Paul wrote to Timothy, "Until I come, devote yourself to the public reading of Scripture, to preaching and to teaching" (1 Timothy 4:13).

One of the first things new converts are encouraged to do is to read the Bible. It is explained that when we receive the Lord Jesus into our lives, we need to learn to hear His voice and speak to Him through prayer. The main way we learn to hear His voice is by reading His Word.

It is important to have a definite, disciplined reading program that will take us through the whole Bible. Here are some interesting facts about a normal reader:

- If you read the Bible fifteen minutes each day, you will read through the whole Bible in less than a year.
- It would take 71 hours to read the whole Bible. The Old Testament would take $52\frac{1}{2}$ hours, the New $18\frac{1}{2}$.
- If you read by chapters, you could read the whole Bible in eighteen weeks by reading ten chapters a day.

Jesus said, "If you hold to my teaching, you are really my disciples. Then you will know the truth, and the truth will set you free" (John 8:31–32).

Studying God's Word

When we study, we exert ourselves and are diligent. When we study God's Word, we search the Scriptures, collecting and collating facts on a theme, doctrine, book or person in order to gain a greater knowledge of God.

Paul commended the Bereans because they "received the message with great eagerness and examined the Scriptures every day to see if what Paul said was true" (Acts 17:11). Although Solomon wrote that "much study wearies the body" (Ecclesiastes

12:12), there is nothing boring or wearisome in making new discoveries of our great God and Savior Jesus Christ.

Memorizing God's Word

The children of Israel were continually exhorted to remember God's Word: "remember all the commands of the LORD, that you may obey them" (Numbers 15:39). "Remember the command that Moses the servant of the LORD gave you" (Joshua 1:13).

Many people claim to have bad memories. Yet in most cases it is not really a bad memory, but an untrained memory. It is highly profitable to store God's Word in our hearts and minds. One of the great blessings of meditating in the Word is that much Scripture becomes stored in our memories, as we will see in a later chapter.

Singing God's Word

Many of the psalms are songs. It is wonderful that so much worship in churches includes singing the Word of God. We can offer God nothing better than what He Himself originated.

Singing Scripture also enables us to memorize it. Many times in the Psalms we are encouraged to sing: "Sing to the LORD, you saints of his; praise his holy name" (Psalm 30:4). "Sing to him a new song; play skillfully, and shout for joy" (Psalm 33:3).

Writing God's Word

Frequently I have been amazed at what I have learned while writing out verses of Scripture in times of study or when preparing a message. Details missed in a reading are often discovered when you write, because every word is written out individually.

Through Moses God gave clear instruction to future kings:

> When he takes the throne of his kingdom, he is to write for himself on a scroll a copy of this law.... It is to be with him, and he is to read it all the days of his life so that he may learn to revere the LORD his God and follow carefully all the words of this law and these decrees.
>
> Deuteronomy 17:18–19

Speaking God's Word

What blessing and exhilaration there is in sharing and talking about God's Word. Whenever we do this, God listens to us!

"Then those who feared the LORD talked with each other, and the LORD listened and heard. A scroll of remembrance was written in his presence concerning those who feared the LORD and honored his name" (Malachi 3:16).

Keep the recording angel busy!

Prayer

Father, thank You for Your Word. Thank You for the many ways by which I can get to know You through it. Help me to discipline my life so that I may do Your will. Please forgive me for any inconsistency in my life or lack of discipline that has robbed me of the knowledge of You, Your ways and Your will.

Teach me Your way, O Lord. I will walk in Your truth. Unite my heart to fear Your name. In Jesus' name, Amen.

Study questions:

1. What is the difference between merely hearing and truly listening to the Word of God?
2. What three things are linked in Scripture with hearing God's Word?
3. Apart from biblical meditation, what other ways do we have of gaining heart knowledge of God?
4. What is the value of memorizing Scripture?
5. Of hearing, reading, studying, memorizing, writing, singing and speaking God's Word, which do you find most helpful? Are there any you neglect?

3

The Blessings of Meditation

> Blessed is the man
>   who does not walk in the counsel of the wicked
> or stand in the way of sinners
>   or sit in the seat of mockers.
> But his delight is in the law of the LORD,
>   and on his law he meditates day and night.
> He is like a tree planted by streams of water,
>   which yields its fruit in season
> and whose leaf does not wither.
>   Whatever he does prospers.
>
> Psalm 1:1–3

Notice how the book of Psalms begins. Right at the start we discover why David had such a capacity for worship and for understanding the ways of God—he had learned to meditate on the Word.

Gladly he passes on the secrets of his devotional practice. Its blessings are as follows.

Happiness

The word "blessed" means happy, even very happy! It could read, "O happy man," or "O, the happiness of that person." Our loving heavenly Father not only wants us to be happy, but tells us how to become so. Other scriptures confirm this: "Blessed is the man who fears the LORD, who finds great delight in his commands" (Psalm 112:1). "Blessed are they whose ways are blameless, who walk according to the law of the LORD. Blessed are they who keep his statutes and seek him with all their heart" (Psalm 119:1–2).

Jesus taught in the Sermon on the Mount that the way to be blessed or happy is to be poor in spirit, to mourn, to be meek, to

16

hunger and thirst after righteousness, to be merciful and pure in heart, to be peacemakers and to bless those who persecute you. These are not human recipes for happiness, but divine ones. Included in the divine recipe is meditation.

Fruitfulness

Not only does God promise happiness to the person who meditates on His Word, but He also promises fruitfulness. Fruit is the evidence of a right relationship, of fellowship with God. It distinguishes between the false and the true.

Jesus said, "By their fruit you will recognize them" (Matthew 7:20). One morning He left Bethany hungry and saw a fig tree that looked attractive from a distance. However, when He approached it He found nothing but leaves—no fruit. Disappointed, He said to the tree, "May you never bear fruit again!" (Matthew 21:19). If it could not satisfy Him, it could never satisfy anyone else.

God's people are likened to trees: "oaks of righteousness, a planting of the LORD for the display of his splendor" (Isaiah 61:3). He comes to us looking for fruit, the evidence of His own life: love, joy, peace, patience, kindness, goodness, faithfulness, gentleness and self-control.

What an encouragement it is that when we meditate continually on God's Word, we are guaranteed to be "like a tree ... which yields its fruit in season."

Freshness

Another promise to those who meditate is that they will not wither. To wither means to fade, become dry or sapless and lose vigor. It is refreshing to meet a saint—young, middle-aged or old—who has never dried up.

I try to meet with a friend of mine once a week, and I always look forward to his visits because he refreshes me. He is a servant of the Lord, and he loves Him. When we meet we talk about the Lord, His Word and His work. The time flies, and having spoken about the Lord we then speak to Him. Although my friend is getting older, he has not lost his vigor or withered spiritually, because he meditates on the Lord's Word.

Paul, in writing to Timothy, said of his friend Onesiphorus, "he often refreshed me" (2 Timothy 1:16). Of other friends he also said, "they refreshed my spirit and yours also" (1 Corinthians 16:18).

What effect do you have on people? Are you a refresher or a refrigerator? Whatever you are, if you make biblical meditation part of your life, you will never wither or dry up, but be an encourager of God's people.

Prosperity

Still another promise to the one who meditates is, "Whatever he does prospers" (Psalm 1:3). This must be one of the greatest promises in the Bible. Imagine a business consultant approaching the principals of a large corporation and offering them a system that, if adopted, would guarantee profit and success! Human systems can fail, but God's guarantees are certain.

When you meditate on God's Word, you can personalize the promise and say, "whatever I do will prosper." That is, whatever we do will have the blessing of the Lord on it.

The greatest riches in the world are the riches of the knowledge of God and His Son, Jesus. It was said of Joseph, "The LORD was with Joseph and he prospered" (Genesis 39:2)—this was when he was a slave in a foreign land. Later, the Bible says that "the LORD was with Joseph and gave him success in whatever he did" (Genesis 39:23)—at that time he was in prison! In the Bible, prosperity is not always linked with material wealth.

A Christian can have riches but be a pauper in the knowledge of God, while some who have little of this world's goods are spiritual millionaires because of their knowledge of God and intimate fellowship with Him.

I remember many years ago ministering in Marseilles, in the south of France, and being taken by a friend to visit a Russian couple. We walked through the poor part of the city, and then climbed some rickety stairs to a small attic apartment. It was one room, sparsely furnished, and there we met the husband and wife who loved the Lord and were radiant.

They sang the great hymn "How Great Thou Art" in Russian, and the room was like a sanctuary. How rich were its occupants! It is not the court that makes the palace, but the presence of the King. We had been with prosperous saints.

There, then, are the blessings that result from meditating on God's Word: happiness, fruitfulness, freshness and prosperity. There is no greater joy on earth than living with the blessing of

God on you. Solomon said, "The blessing of the LORD brings wealth, and he adds no trouble to it" (Proverbs 10:22).

Prayer

Father, thank You for all the blessings You have already brought into my life, and thank You for all the blessings You promise me. I desire to be a fruitful Christian, and thank You for choosing me so that I may bring forth lasting fruit. I confess that without You I can do nothing, but with You I can do all things. Save me from withering, but help me through Your Word and by Your Spirit to be full of Your life, peace and joy.

As You offer these wonderful blessings to those who meditate in your Word, continue to teach me how this can be part of my life. In Jesus' name. Amen.

Study questions:

1. Can you give your own definition of the word "blessed"? According to the Bible, how do we become blessed?
2. What does it mean to bear fruit spiritually?
3. Do you know any Christians who are particularly good examples of freshness and who refresh the church?
4. What is God's perspective on prosperity? How does this apply to us?
5. Are you personally blessed, fruitful, unwithered and prosperous? Do you want to be?

4

The Condition of Separation

Now that we have reviewed the wonderful promises given to the one who meditates on God's Word, let us look at the conditions for their fulfillment.

This is a simple rule to follow when you read the Bible: Pay attention to what God says He will do, but also pay attention to what He tells us to do. If we do what He instructs us, He will always fulfill His promises. The pattern is, "If my people ... will ... then will I ... " (2 Chronicles 7:14).

Separation from Sin

The first condition is to break our alliance with the ungodly, the sinner and the scornful:

> Blessed is the man
>   who does not walk in the counsel of the wicked
> or stand in the way of sinners
>   or sit in the seat of mockers.
>
> Psalm 1:1

Paul voices the same thing:

> Do not be yoked together with unbelievers. For what do righteousness and wickedness have in common? Or what fellowship can light have with darkness? What harmony is there between Christ and Belial? What does a believer have in common with an unbeliever? What agreement is there between the temple of God and idols? For we are the temple of the living God. As God has said, "I will live with them and walk among them, and I will be their God, and they will be my people."
>
> > "Therefore come out from them
> > and be separate,
> >
> > says the Lord.

> Touch no unclean thing,
> and I will receive you."
> "I will be a Father to you,
> and you will be my sons and daughters,
>   says the Lord Almighty."
>   2 Corinthians 6:14–18

Although we are called to separation, we are not called to isolation. Jesus was called a "friend of ... 'sinners'" (Matthew 11:19; Luke 7:34). But in friendships with those who, as yet, do not know the saving grace of the Lord Jesus, we must not be involved with their sins. If we walk in the counsel of the ungodly, we will soon be sitting with them.

Instead of allowing the world to influence us, we should influence others to follow God—we should be signposts pointing to the Lord Jesus. Jesus prayed for His disciples:

> My prayer is not that you take them out of the world but that you protect them from the evil one. They are not of the world, even as I am not of it. Sanctify them by the truth; your word is truth. As you sent me into the world, I have sent them into the world.... May they be brought to complete unity to let the world know that you sent me and have loved them.
>   John 17:15–18, 23

The Word either separates people from the world, or the world separates people from the Word. The devil told Adam and Eve that if they obeyed God they would be the losers, and he is still whispering that lie today. But God says, "Blessed is the man"—very happy are those who are separated from the world.

The world is not something merely external: gambling, immorality, drunkenness, cheating and so on. The world is unregenerate human nature, whenever or wherever it is found, either in the church or outside the church. So our warfare is against the spirit of the world. Whether this is manifested in obvious outward ways or in subtle, refined ways, we must recognize and repudiate it.

James wrote emphatically, "You adulterous people, don't you know that friendship with the world is hatred towards God? Anyone who chooses to be a friend of the world becomes an enemy of God" (James 4:4). Choose to be separated from sin and joined to God. Choose to love God and not the world. Embrace the cross of our Lord Jesus and stand with the apostle Paul as he declares, "May I never boast except in the cross of our Lord Jesus

Christ, through which the world has been crucified to me, and I to the world" (Galatians 6:14).

Thank God that part of the saving work of the cross is that it separates us from the world. The twentieth-century prophet Dr. A. W. Tozer wrote:

> The old cross would have no truck with the world. For Adam's proud flesh it meant the end of the journey....
>
> The old cross is a symbol of death. It stands for the abrupt and violent end of a human being. The man in Roman times who took up his cross and started down the road had already said farewell to his friends. He was not coming back. The cross made no compromise, modified nothing, it slew all of the man, completely and for good. It struck cruel and hard, and when it had finished its work, the man was no more.
>
> The race of Adam is under death sentence. There is no commutation, and no escape ... our message is not a compromise, but an ultimatum.[1]

What are the results of this death and separation from the old life? Friendship with God, peace, true happiness, intimate fellowship. "I will be a Father to you, and you will be my sons and daughters, says the Lord Almighty."

Prayer

Father, I want to glory in the cross of the Lord Jesus. I acknowledge that it separates me from the world. I choose not to walk in the counsel of the ungodly, or stand in the way of sinners, or sit in the seat of mockers, and I thank You that You are able to keep me from evil. I want to know the fear of God, which is to hate evil.

Please give me a continual love for those who do not know You, and let my life and witness speak of You. Please reveal yourself to me through Your Word, and let it have an abiding place in my life, so that I can be clean through the words You speak to me, as Jesus promised. Amen.

Study questions:

1. What does God promise us when we obey His words to us?
2. How do we break our alliance with the ungodly, the sinful and the scornful?
3. How can we follow Jesus in the way we relate to "sinners"?

4. What is "the world" as defined by the Scriptures?
5. Do you personally know the meaning of the cross in terms of death and separation from the old life?

Note

1. A. W. Tozer, *The Old Cross and The New,* article published by The Alliance Witness in 1946.

5

The Condition of Delight

The second essential the psalmist gives for meditation is to "delight ... in the law of the LORD" (Psalm 1:2). To delight simply means to take pleasure. This will be an increasing experience as you meditate, as new discoveries are made in the Word of the wonders of God and His ways.

Delighting in His Word

When the Lord is our delight, then we will delight in His Word. This pleasure will increase as we continue to hear His voice and grow in the knowledge of Him. Meditation is not a technical exercise but a loving relationship in which He communes with us and we commune with Him.

There is abundant evidence in the Psalms that God's Word gave David absolute joy. We can see this especially in Psalm 119, where he speaks out of the depth of his personal experience:

> I delight in your commands,
> because I love them.
>
> verse 47

> Your statutes are my delight;
> they are my counselors.
>
> verse 24

> The law from your mouth is more precious to me
> than thousands of pieces of silver and gold.
>
> verse 72

> How sweet are your words to my taste,
> sweeter than honey to my mouth!
>
> verse 103

> Your promises have been thoroughly tested,
> and your servant loves them.
>
> verse 140
>
> I rejoice in your promise
> like one who finds great spoil.
>
> verse 162

David clearly did not find God's Word dry or boring. Why? We will consider two main reasons.

Delighting in the Lord

We cannot delight in the Word without delighting in its Author. As it was with David, so it should be with us. He loved God, who was his pleasure, his joy, his life.

David made a choice to love God. He determined that it would be so, and so it was. He said, "I will be glad and rejoice in your love" (Psalm 31:7).

One of the principal ways of showing our love for God, and our delight in Him, is to discover and fulfill the things that give Him pleasure. Here are some of these:

Loving Those Who Love God
In Proverbs, the voice of Wisdom speaks: "I love those who love me, and those who seek me find me" (Proverbs 8:17).

Obeying God
Jesus said, "Whoever has my commands and obeys them, he is the one who loves me. He who loves me will be loved by my Father, and I too will love him and show myself to him" (John 14:21).

Following after Righteousness
Solomon wrote, "The LORD detests the way of the wicked but he loves those who pursue righteousness" (Proverbs 15:9).

Serving God Rightly
Paul wrote, "For the kingdom of God is not a matter of eating and drinking, but of righteousness, peace and joy in the Holy Spirit, because anyone who serves Christ in this way is pleasing to God and approved by men" (Romans 14:17–18).

Joyless service gives God no pleasure. The Lord said of Israel, "Because you did not serve the LORD your God joyfully and gladly in the time of prosperity, therefore ... you will serve the enemies the LORD sends against you" (Deuteronomy 28:47–48).

Giving Cheerfully to God

Like serving, giving must be done with joy. Paul wrote to the Corinthians, "Each man should give what he has decided in his heart to give, not reluctantly or under compulsion, for God loves a cheerful giver" (2 Corinthians 9:7). John McNeil, a Scottish minister, described a cheerful giver as a person in church who shouted, "Hallelujah, here comes the collection plate!"

Praying with a Right Heart

How God loves to hear us, and what delight He receives when we pray with a sincere, believing heart. "The LORD detests the sacrifice of the wicked, but the prayer of the upright pleases him" (Proverbs 15:8).

Praising God with a Right Heart

How good David was at this. He said, "I will praise God's name in song and glorify him with thanksgiving. This will please the LORD more than an ox" (Psalm 69:30–31).

Having a Broken and Contrite Heart

God hates sin, but He is full of mercy for the truly repentant. After David committed adultery with Bathsheba and ordered the death of her husband, Uriah, he confessed his sin with humility and brokenness. And God received him, just as the prodigal's father delighted to see the wanderer coming back home.

David said:

> You do not delight in sacrifice, or I would bring it;
>   you do not take pleasure in burnt offerings.
> The sacrifices of God are a broken spirit;
>   a broken and contrite heart,
> O God, you will not despise.

> Psalm 51:16–17

Seeking to Please God in Everything

Giving pleasure and delight to God can be summed up in the words of Paul:

> For this reason, since the day we heard about you, we have not stopped praying for you and asking God to fill you with the

knowledge of his will through all spiritual wisdom and understanding. And we pray this in order that you may live a life worthy of the Lord and may please him in every way: bearing fruit in every good work, growing in the knowledge of God, being strengthened with all power according to his glorious might so that you may have great endurance and patience.

Colossians 1:9–11

Delighting in the Will of God

If we delight in the Lord and His Word, we will also delight in His will. David said, "I desire to do your will, O my God; your law is within my heart" (Psalm 40:8). The will of God is not meant to be a mere obligation but a pleasure. It is not just something good but is the best. There is no real joy, lasting peace or fulfillment for the child of God outside His will.

We should therefore yield ourselves totally to Him, both to know and to do His bidding. In fact, we cannot truly know His will unless we are surrendered to it, as Paul explained to the Christians in Rome when he wrote:

Therefore, I urge you, brothers, in view of God's mercy, to offer your bodies as living sacrifices, holy and pleasing to God—this is your spiritual act of worship. Do not conform any longer to the pattern of this world, but be transformed by the renewing of your mind. Then you will be able to test and approve what God's will is—his good, pleasing and perfect will.

Romans 12:1–2

Choosing to do the will of God is essential. Jesus said, "If anyone chooses to do God's will, he will find out whether my teaching comes from God or whether I speak on my own" (John 7:17).

Submission to God's will causes a free flow of revelation through the Word, as we borrow the words of the Lord Jesus to make them our own desire: "I seek not to please myself but him who sent me" (John 5:30).

Pleasing the Lord

Be still before the Lord now. Tell Him you want to delight in Him and in His will and His Word. Ponder some of the things that please Him and make them applicable in your life. Examples of these follow.

Loving Those Who Love God

Is there someone you do not love? Do you nurse any resentment, bitterness or unforgiveness? Confess it to the Lord and pray God's blessing on the people concerned.

Obeying God

He has promised to manifest Himself to those who obey Him. Is there any disobedience in your life? Choose to be obedient and thus give Him joy.

Following after Righteousness

Tell God you choose to do the right thing and to be honest and upright in all your dealings with Him and with other people.

Giving

Choose to please the Lord by giving to Him generously and cheerfully, as an expression of your love for Him.

Praying and Praising

It is wonderful that we can please God by our praying and praising. He hears us and delights in our praises. Are you doing these things?

Delighting to Do His Will

Yield yourself completely to Him by presenting your whole life and body. When He has our body, He has everything, because housed within us is our soul and spirit. Now take the words of David and make them yours: "I desire to do your will, O my God" (Psalm 40:8).

Prayer

My Father, I come to You in the name of the Lord Jesus, realizing that without You I can do nothing. I want to give You pleasure and joy by delighting in You, Your will and Your Word.

Here is my body, which I present to You. I know it has already been bought by the precious blood of Jesus, and that I am only giving You what is rightfully Yours. Please help me by the power of the Spirit to love what You love and hate what You hate. Save me from joyless service and a powerless life. Help me to love all who love You, to be obedient to all that You tell me, to live uprightly and give cheerfully. May my prayers and praise be acceptable in Your sight.

Thank You for all that You will reveal of Yourself as I learn to meditate on Your Word. I want to hear the voice of the Beloved to my heart and receive the comfort and guidance of the Good Shepherd. I want to receive the loving instruction from my perfect Teacher and truth from You who are the Light of the world.

You are glorious and majestic. I delight in You, and praise, thank and worship You. Amen.

Study questions:

1. What was David's attitude to the Word of God?
2. Explain some of the ways we have to show our delight in the Lord.
3. How can following the will of God be a pleasure to us?
4. What does the author mean by saying that we cannot truly know God's will without surrendering to it?
5. What aspects of pleasing the Lord come naturally to you? Which are a struggle?

6

A Definition of Meditation

Now let us define meditation, by considering what it really is.

The Inner Reception of Truth

Meditation is the devotional practice of pondering the words of a verse or verses of Scripture with a receptive heart. Through meditating, we allow the Holy Spirit to take the written Word and apply it as living Word into our inner being. As divine truth is imparted to us, it inevitably brings forth a response to God.

Meditation has been described as "the digestive faculty of the soul." Jeremiah wrote:

> When your words came, I ate them;
>> they were my joy and my heart's delight,
> for I bear your name,
>> O LORD God Almighty.

Jeremiah 15:16

Because meditation is inwardly receiving the Word of God, it is often illustrated by eating or feeding. God spoke to Ezekiel:

> "You must speak my words to them, whether they listen or fail to listen, for they are rebellious. But you, son of man, listen to what I say to you ... open your mouth and eat what I give you."
>
> Then I looked, and I saw a hand stretched out to me. In it was a scroll, which he unrolled before me. On both sides of it were written words of lament....
>
> And he said to me, "Son of man, eat what is before you, eat this scroll; then go and speak to the house of Israel." So I opened my mouth, and he gave me the scroll to eat.
>
> Then he said to me, "Son of man, eat this scroll I am giving you and fill your stomach with it." So I ate it, and it tasted as sweet as honey in my mouth.

Ezekiel 2:7–3:3

The word "meditate" is taken from the Latin root *meditari,* similar to the Latin *medicari,* from which we get the word "medicate." Medicine in the bottle has no effect. It has to be received internally—normally three times a day! Meditation, like medicine, has healing properties.

In Exodus 16 we read of God's provision of manna for the children of Israel. Here was "bread from heaven" (John 6:31) to feed and sustain them. So what did people do when they saw it? Did they admire, analyze or dissect it? No. They ate it and inwardly received it.

More Truth—More Life

Jesus made this wonderful statement: "The Spirit gives life; the flesh counts for nothing. The words I have spoken to you are spirit and they are life" (John 6:63). Therefore, the more of the Word we receive inwardly, the more life we receive. This is one of the basic principles for spiritual growth. God's words are living words, spirit and life words, and as they are imparted to us, our spiritual capacity is increased. It is important to understand this vital truth.

Let us look at what Peter says about the value of God's Word:

> His divine power has given us everything we need for life and godliness through our knowledge of him who called us by his own glory and goodness. Through these he has given us his very great and precious promises, so that through them you may participate in the divine nature and escape the corruption in the world caused by evil desires.
>
> 2 Peter 1:3–4

Peter is saying that when you believe a promise of God, you receive something of God Himself, something of His divine nature.

For instance, if people came to faith in a meeting, the Holy Spirit would have convicted them of their sin as they heard the great news of God's love and Jesus' death on the cross. Somehow they had begun to take hold of "very great and precious promises," perhaps John 3:36, "Whoever believes in the Son has eternal life."

What happened when this word was believed and inwardly received? They were given everlasting life, something of the divine nature—they received something of God Himself!

Another promise I take to the Lord every morning is, "If any of you lacks wisdom, he should ask God, who gives generously to all without finding fault, and it will be given to him" (James 1:5).

What happens when this promise is believed and inwardly received? As I admit to God that my human wisdom is insufficient to do His will, to make the right decisions, to cope with the various and unexpected circumstances of everyday life, and as I ask for His wisdom, He imparts His wisdom to me. Wisdom is part of the divine nature, so the more I receive of Him and from Him, the more I grow. The more I grow, the more of His life will be manifested through me. Through meditation there is a continual impartation of His Word, His truth, His life.

More Truth—More Light

Not only is there life in truth, but there is also light. David said, "The unfolding of your words gives light; it gives understanding to the simple" (Psalm 119:130). Therefore, the more of God's Word we receive inwardly, the more light we receive. The phrase "the unfolding of your words" is translated in the King James Version as "the entrance of your words." We are not merely looking at truth or admiring it, but inwardly receiving it—it enters us.

This is what happens in true meditation. Jesus said, "You are the light of the world" (Matthew 5:14). We will shine brighter and brighter as we allow His Word to enter our hearts. That same Word will illuminate our way. "Your word is a lamp to my feet and a light for my path" (Psalm 119:105).

Revelation

Meditation is receiving revelation through God's Word. All truth that vitally affects our lives comes not merely by explanation, but by revelation.

Many of us have read or heard truths we believed in our heads but failed to understand in our hearts. Then one day a light went on and we said, "Now I see it." What happened? Was there an increase in our IQ? No. We received revelation, and that truth became meaningful and personal in our lives.

Verses of Scripture can be like flowers that have closed their petals because the sun has gone down. We can still admire them as part of God's creative miracle, but much of their beauty is hidden. However, in the morning when the sun rises, the flowers begin to open towards the light, so we can appreciate their full beauty, color and detail.

In the same way we can value Scripture but fail to behold its beauty and detail. However, when we meditate, seeking divine illumination by the Sun of Righteousness, revelation and insight come to us. These impart knowledge of the Creator, knowledge we now become stewards of.

We are wholly dependent on the Holy Spirit to give us this revelation. Paul said:

> "No eye has seen,
>   no ear has heard,
> no mind has conceived
>   what God has prepared for those who love him"—

> but God has revealed it to us by his Spirit. The Spirit searches all things, even the deep things of God. For who among men knows the thoughts of a man except the man's spirit within him? In the same way no one knows the thoughts of God except the Spirit of God.
>
> 1 Corinthians 2:9–11

Jesus promised the disciples that when the Spirit of truth came, He would guide us into all truth. How wonderful to have the greatest Teacher both in and with us, to reveal truth to us.

Summary

Meditation is the practice of pondering, considering and reflecting on verses of Scripture. It must be done in total dependence on the Holy Spirit to give revelation of truth and meaning, as we obediently receive and respond to it. If we have an attitude of humility and trust, this truth brings life and light as it is imparted to our inner beings.

Meditation is inwardly receiving truth. It is feeding on Christ, who is the Living Word and the Bread of Life. Through it we grow more Christlike and His brightness becomes increasingly evident to those around us.

Prayer

Father, by Your grace and mercy I am a child of God. I thank You that You delight to reveal Yourself through Your Word. I come to

You, dependent and childlike, desiring to receive and obey the revelation of Your will. Let Your Word truly be a lamp to my feet and a light to my path.

Study questions:

1. How is meditating like eating? How is it like taking medicine?
2. How does our spiritual capacity increase as we take in more of the Word?
3. Why are we able to fulfill our calling to be "the light of the world" as we meditate?
4. What is the difference between explanation and revelation?
5. Do you experience life and light being imparted to your inner being as you feed on the Scriptures?

7

The Results of Meditation

The Word of God is a treasure that produces great riches in and from the lives of those who meditate on it. The translators of the King James Version of the Bible wrote a letter to the king when they submitted their new version:

> But among all our joys, there was no one that more filled our hearts, than the blessed continuance of the preaching of God's sacred word among us; which is that inestimable treasure, which excelleth all the riches of the earth; because the fruit thereof extendeth itself, not only to the time spent in this transitory world, but directeth and disposeth men unto that eternal happiness which is above in heaven.

How true. As we receive the Word it does "extend itself," because it is life and produces life. That life is manifested in those who have chosen to be those who do what the Word says, not merely listen to it (James 1:22)—in the words of the King James Version, are "doers of the word, and not hearers only."

The Fear of the Lord and the Knowledge of God

David, having known the blessedness of meditating on God's Word, obviously passed on to his son Solomon some of this treasure. In describing the search for wisdom, Solomon gives a clear definition of meditation and its results:

> My son, if you accept my words
>   and store up my commands within you,
> turning your ear to wisdom
>   and applying your heart to understanding,
> and if you call out for insight
>   and cry aloud for understanding,

> and if you look for it as for silver
> and search for it as for hidden treasure,
> then you will understand the fear of the L<small>ORD</small>
> and find the knowledge of God.

Proverbs 2:1–5

The greatest product of meditation is the fear of the Lord and the knowledge of God. "The fear of the L<small>ORD</small> is the beginning of knowledge" (Proverbs 1:7), and through it we acquire wisdom. Solomon reminds us that to acquire this knowledge we must receive the Word, treasure and keep it within us, and continually seek for more.

Respect for God's Ways

Meditation brings a respect for God's ways. David said:

> I meditate on your precepts
> and consider your ways.
> I delight in your decrees;
> I will not neglect your word.

Psalm 119:15–16

As he pondered the commands of God and meditated on them, he showed full respect for them and joyous obedience to them.

Strength to Resist Temptation

David received much opposition in his life both from enemies outside and enemies within. He was the object of criticism and judgment, but testified that meditation prevented him from wrong reactions. He said, "Though rulers sit together and slander me, your servant will meditate on your decrees" (Psalm 119:23).

The more the Word of God is in us, the better equipped we are to resist sinning. God's decree for His children is to follow His will, and we come to know His will through His Word. David learned to retaliate not by defending himself or attacking his opponents, but by acting according to the Word of God within him.

Increased Love for the Word

The more we eat and taste of the Word of God, the more our love for it grows. Our appetites for it also grow larger. When we eat the best, we develop a preference for it and lose our taste for what is inferior. Isaiah wrote, "He will eat curds and honey when he knows enough to reject the wrong and choose the right" (Isaiah 7:15).

David's meditation in the Word and obedience to it produced an ever-increasing love for God and for what God says. He expressed this: "I delight in your commands because I love them. I lift up my hands to your commands, which I love, and I meditate on your decrees" (Psalm 119:47–48). "Oh, how I love your law! I meditate on it all day long" (Psalm 119:97).

This too will be your experience as one who meditates on the Word of God.

Growth in Understanding

Again we quote David:

> I have more insight than all my teachers,
>   for I meditate on your statutes.
> I have more understanding than the elders,
>   for I obey your precepts.
>
> Psalm 119:99–100

David did not say that he had more knowledge than his teachers, but that he had more insight and understanding. What is the use of knowledge if you do not understand it? Paul reminded us that mere knowledge "puffs up" (1 Corinthians 8:1).

Solomon often used three words in the book of Proverbs: knowledge, understanding and wisdom. *Knowledge* is being acquainted with the facts. *Understanding* is having insight as to what the facts mean. *Wisdom* is the ability to apply what we know and understand to our life and circumstances. David's testimony was that meditation gave him understanding.

A Response to God

All real meditation brings a response to God. Whether the response is confession, praise, thanksgiving, worship, prayer, intercession or action, it is very valuable.

The wonderful thing is that while we receive more from God, God receives more from us. You will know when you have completed a meditation because in some way you have responded to God.

A great saint called George Müller was challenged in the 1830s by the faithlessness of many of his contemporaries. He longed, in his words, for "visible proof" that God is the same faithful Father as ever He was.

God directed George Müller to initiate a program to house and care for orphans in the city of Bristol in southwest England. He looked solely to God to supply every need, and the story is a vibrant testimony to God's faithfulness. Müller testified to the great blessing meditation brought to his life:

> It has pleased the Lord to teach me a truth, the benefit of which I have not lost for fourteen years. I saw more clearly than ever that the first business to which I ought to attend every day, was to have my soul happy in the Lord. The first thing to be concerned about was not how much I might serve the Lord, but how I might get my soul in a happy state, and how my inner man might be nourished. I might seek truth to set before the unconverted, I might seek to benefit believers, I might seek to relieve the distressed, and I might in other ways seek to behave myself as it becomes a child of God in this world, and yet, not being happy in the Lord, and not being strengthened in the inner man day by day, all this might not be attended to in the right spirit.
>
> Before this time my practice had been to give myself to prayer after having dressed in the morning. Now I saw the most important thing I had to do was to give myself to the reading of the word of God and to meditate on it, thus my heart might be comforted, encouraged, warned, reproved, instructed, and that thus, by means of the word of God, my heart might be brought into experimental communion with the Lord.
>
> I began therefore to meditate on the New Testament from the beginning, early in the morning. The first thing I did after having asked in a few words the Lord's blessing upon his word, was to begin to meditate on the word, searching as it were every verse to get a blessing out of it ... not for the sake of public ministry, nor preaching, but for obtaining food for my soul.
>
> The result I found to be inevitably this. After a few minutes my soul had been led to confession, or thanksgiving, or intercession, or supplication, yet it turned almost immediately to prayer. When thus, I had for a while been making confession, or inter-cession or supplication, or having given thanks, I go to the next words of the verse, turning all as I go into prayer for myself or others, as the word may lead to it, but still continually keeping before me that food for my own soul as the object of my meditation.
>
> The difference, then, between my present practice and my

former is this. Formerly when I arose, I began to pray as soon as possible, and generally spent all my time before breakfast in prayer, or almost all the time. At all events I almost always began with prayer, except when I felt my soul to be more than usually barren, in which case I would read the word. But what was the result? I often spent a quarter of an hour, or half an hour, or even an hour on my knees before having been conscious to myself of having derived comfort, encouragement, humbling of the soul etc., and often after having suffered much from wandering thoughts . . . I only then began to really pray. I scarcely ever suffer in this way now, for my heart, being brought into experimental fellowship with God, I speak to my Father about the things he has brought to me in his precious word. It often astonishes me that I did not sooner see this point.[1]

George Müller proved that meditation was a life-changing devotional practice, always bringing a response from God.

Meditation Day and Night

Another product of meditation is that what God has said to us does not disappear but keeps returning. David was not shut away in some cloister—he was a busy king, father, husband, soldier and statesman. God also told Joshua to meditate "day and night" (Joshua 1:8), and Joshua too was busy.

Meditation is sometimes illustrated by a cow chewing the cud. Once in Switzerland I went for a walk in the countryside and came to a field with cows in it, bells tied to their necks. As I studied them, I learned some lessons.

First, I noticed that they chewed the cud only when they were resting. Obviously, there would have been no cud unless they had first eaten, but what they had eaten kept coming back to be chewed again. They would chew a bit more on it, swallow, and soon it would come back again.

So it is with meditation. You can meditate on a verse in the morning, and during the day or night it keeps returning so that you can "chew" on it a bit more!

In another place I saw a mother cow chewing the cud while her calf was feeding from her. I realized that our ability to feed others is dependent on what we ourselves have received.

No doubt David learned to meditate when he was a shepherd, spending days and nights out in the open fields, contemplating the wonders of God and His creation. He said, "My eyes stay open through the watches of the night, that I may meditate on your promises" (Psalm 119:148).

What an encouragement to meditate. It produces the fear of the Lord and the knowledge of God; it causes us to respect the ways of God; it strengthens us to resist temptation; it produces an increased love for God and His Word; it gives us understanding; it brings forth response to God; it keeps coming back.

Prayer

Father, I want to thank You for the treasure-house of Your Word, containing revelation that no wealth on earth could buy. I want to be a diligent seeker of truth, not only receiving knowledge but also understanding. Thank You that Your Word helps me to walk in Your ways.

Strengthen me to resist temptation so that I do not react in the flesh. I praise You that my love for You and Your Word will increase. Like David, I choose to delight myself in Your commandments, and incline my heart to Your ways. Amen.

Study questions:

1. Why is it important for us to do what the Word says, not only to listen to it?
2. What results can we expect from meditating on God's Word?
3. How do we know when we have completed a meditation?
4. What did George Müller learn about meditating on Scripture?
5. How can we take in God's Word day and night, in both an active and a more restful way?

Note

1. Excerpt from a tract produced by Osterhouse Publishing House, Minneapolis.

8

The Practice of Meditation, Part I

Having considered the importance, blessing, conditions, definition and results of meditation, we now come to its practice—the "how-to."

The story in Luke's gospel of Jesus, after His resurrection, meeting up with the two disciples on the Emmaus road illustrates certain truths that need to be applied as we practice meditation.

Sitting with the Lord

When the Lord accepted the invitation into the disciples' home, it is recorded that He was "at the table with them" (Luke 24:30). This is the first requirement: to sit relaxed before the Lord. This obviously does not mean that we can only meditate when sitting, but indicates the importance of an attitude of restful waiting on Him.

We may have been busy with many things, and have many things on our minds, but now we come to meet with Him and hear His voice, through His Word. We need to put aside all distracting thoughts, and pray as Wesley did:

> Expand thy wings celestial dove,
> Brood o'er our nature's night,
> On our disordered spirits move,
> And let there be light.[1]

Solomon said, "I delight to sit in his shade, and his fruit is sweet to my taste" (Song of Songs 2:3).

Before Jesus fed the multitude He commanded them first to sit. We need to ensure that our hearts are right with Him, so sin must be confessed. Then we can come with restful confidence in the knowledge that as we draw near to Him, He draws near to us.

Hearing the Voice of God

How important it is to know and recognize His voice. The impressions we get as we meditate come from four main sources:

- other people
- ourselves
- the devil
- God

While meditating we are usually on our own, so are less influenced by other people. Because we want God's thoughts and not our own, it is important to discern between the different voices as we prepare to hear from God. How can we do this?

Impressions from Ourselves

Proverbs 3:5–6 tells us:

> Trust in the LORD with all your heart
>   and lean not on your own understanding;
> in all your ways acknowledge him,
>   and he will make your paths straight.

Bring this as a prayer to God, with a sincere heart. Tell Him that you come trusting Him to speak to you through the Word. Affirm that you are not depending on your own understanding or intellect, because "He who trusts in himself is a fool" (Proverbs 28:26).

Tell God that you do acknowledge Him in all your ways, and trust Him to direct your paths. Thank Him that you are going to hear His voice. We are totally dependent on Him and His Holy Spirit to help us receive His thoughts.

Impressions from the Devil

Although we have an enemy, the Lord Jesus has defeated him. Nevertheless, we are not ignorant of his devices. The devil does not want Christians to be strong through the knowledge of God. But there is protection from any inroads he would seek to make, and we can stand against him in the name of the Lord.

Arm yourselves with these scriptures, and use them with faith whenever you are conscious of the enemy's attacks or diversions. They are provided for our protection.

Submit yourselves, then, to God. Resist the devil, and he will flee from you.

James 4:7

You, dear children, are from God and have overcome them, because the one who is in you is greater than the one who is in the world.

1 John 4:4

> They overcame him
> by the blood of the Lamb
> and by the word of their testimony;
> they did not love their lives so much
> as to shrink from death.

Revelation 12:11

Humble yourselves, therefore, under God's mighty hand, that he may lift you up in due time. Cast all your anxiety on him because he cares for you. Be self-controlled and alert. Your enemy the devil prowls around like a roaring lion looking for someone to devour. Resist him, standing firm in the faith, because you know that your brothers throughout the world are undergoing the same kind of sufferings.

1 Peter 5:6–9

Put on the full armor of God so that you can take your stand against the devil's schemes.... Stand firm then, with the belt of truth buckled round your waist, with the breastplate of righteousness in place, and with your feet fitted with the readiness that comes from the gospel of peace. In addition to all this, take up the shield of faith, with which you can extinguish all the flaming arrows of the evil one. Take the helmet of salvation and the sword of the Spirit, which is the word of God. And pray in the Spirit on all occasions with all kinds of prayers and requests. With this in mind, be alert and always keep on praying for all the saints.

Ephesians 6:11, 14–18

When we come against the enemy, submitted to God, and in the name of the Lord Jesus resisting the devil, then he must flee. We do not need to fear receiving impressions from him. Praise God for His victory, that in Him we can be continual overcomers.

Impressions from God

Having dealt with other sources, we now trust the Lord to speak to us through His Word, and know that He will. All that He says will glorify His name, causing us to worship Him. It will always agree with the biblical revelation of God.

The impressions we receive from God will impart knowledge of Him. They will not cause us to be "puffed up" with knowledge, but will enable us to love Him and others more. What He says will be true, honest, just, pure, lovely and of good report. It will be the voice of the good Shepherd that we, His sheep, will recognize and follow.

God's Word will be the joy of our heart. We will come to Him, saying, "Speak, for your servant is listening" (1 Samuel 3:10), knowing that we will never be disappointed. We will go from our time of meditation with a sense of awe because we have heard the voice of the Almighty. His Word will linger and return, because He has imparted it to us. It will become part of the very fiber of our being, and bring life, light and the knowledge of the Holy.

Christ the Giver

The Emmaus story confirms that we are completely dependent on the Lord to feed us from His Word. As the disciples sat at the table with Jesus, He took the bread, He blessed it, He broke it and He gave it. They sat and received it.

So it is in meditation. We read a verse or verses, and then ponder what we have read, but He is the one who gives revelation and understanding. Meditation is not an intellectual exercise, though God does not bypass our minds. It is not just puzzling over what the Scripture means, nor is it delving into a commentary to get another's thoughts (good as this may be). It is allowing the Master to impart to us personally from His loving heart.

The result was that "their eyes were opened and they recognized him" (Luke 24:31). They received not merely a revelation of truth, but a revelation of Christ. Although He disappeared from their sight, the wonder and joy remained, and with burning hearts they rushed to Jerusalem to share with others what they had received from Him.

Application

Consider the various points of this chapter, and then make them a matter of prayer.

Sitting with the Lord

Some, because of their temperament, find this easier than others. Some have a placid disposition, and others a more restless one—but both need the help of the Lord. Share with the Lord any difficulties you have in this realm, and tell Him what help you need. Why not write them down?

_____

_____

_____

_____

_____

_____

Hearing God's Voice

Have you had difficulty here? Tell the Lord about it, and apply the teaching of this chapter, looking to Him and not "leaning on your own understanding." Take God's protection against the enemy. Use the Word of God against him, submit yourself to God, stand, resist and take the place of victory in Jesus.

Looking to Jesus

Acknowledge that He is the giver of "every good and perfect gift" (James 1:17). He is the one who takes the Word, blesses, breaks and gives it to you. Ask Him to help you to receive it.

Prayer

Father, open my eyes that I may see wonderful things out of Your Word. Teach me to rest in You and hear Your voice. Thank You that because Christ is in me, and I am in Him, I can resist all the power of the enemy. Feed me from Your Word, that I may know You. Amen.

Study questions:

1. In what way was Jesus' encounter with the disciples at Emmaus a pattern for our meeting with Him through Scripture?
2. Why is it important that we hear from God, not just from our own thoughts?
3. How do we resist the devil?

4. What are the characteristics of impressions from God?
5. How easy do you find it to wait quietly before the Lord?

Note

1. From the hymn, *Come, Holy Ghost, Our Hearts Inspire,* by Charles Wesley, 1740.

9

The Practice of Meditation, Part II

Having seen the need of a restful, but attentive, attitude towards the Lord, with disciplined thoughts, resisting the work of the enemy, we now look at some important questions about preparing to meditate.

What Should I Meditate on?

Because God knows us, our needs and situations, so well, it is important to ask Him. In doing so we are again acknowledging Him in all our ways. Sometimes in reading the Word, verses are quickened to us, and we have a desire to meditate on them, so that we may receive all that God wishes to reveal to us. That is good. However, because God is a God of order and because the Bible is put together in a special way, a systematic, verse-by-verse method of meditation is strongly recommended.

The first step is to ask God to put into our minds the book of the Bible in which He wants us to meditate. Then, starting at chapter 1, verse 1, we proceed through the whole of that book. It may take six months, or a year, to complete meditating through a particular book.

So that you may start right, discover now where God wants you to meditate. We are going to put into practice the teaching of the previous chapter, by asking God to put into your mind the book in the Bible in which He wants you to meditate. Are you ready? Tell the Lord that you give up your own thoughts and choice of books, and that you only want His will. Now pray your own prayer, or follow this one: "Father, I come to You as Your child, having chosen to meditate on Your Word each day. I surrender my own choice and ask You to put into my mind the book in which You want me to meditate. Thank You. Amen."

Be still . . . the first book that comes to your mind is the answer. Now write down the book He has given you.

The Lord has shown me to meditate in _____.

Date _____

Well done! When you have completed the book, ask the Lord what the next one should be. Do not forget God's promise that the one who meditates will be blessed, fruitful and prosperous.

How Long Should I Meditate?

Meditate until you have received from the Lord. Initially, set aside at least fifteen minutes. Remember that the word we receive will continually return to our minds, just like the cud a cow chews. The Lord can give revelation of truth immediately, or it can take longer. He knows the pressures on us, and He rewards those who earnestly seek Him. There is little progress in Christian living without the discipline of time with God.

When Is the Best Time to Meditate?

We cannot be dogmatic or legalistic in answering this question. The best time to meditate is when we can sit unhurriedly with the Lord.

A mother with young children may well not find much time until about midmorning. People on shift work will have to adapt according to their work schedule. Nevertheless, because we have chosen to "seek first his kingdom and his righteousness" (Matthew 6:33), meditation is going to have a priority in our lives, together with other means of approaching the Word.

There is no doubt that where it is possible, first thing in the morning is the best time to meditate. Some feel more relaxed in the evening, but as someone has said, "Why tune up the fiddle when the concert is over?" Determine what the best time is for you, and discipline your life accordingly.

What If I Am Unsure Whether the Thoughts Are Mine or His?

Sometimes this question may come to your mind. A simple way to deal with it is to ask the Lord to remove it if it is not from Him.

Ask Him to confirm it if it is! Our God is such a wonderful teacher and friend, and He will respond to our requests when He sees we really want to know Him and do His will.

When doubts arise, certain questions can be asked to test whether it is from God. They include:

- Does it glorify God and exalt the Lord Jesus?
- Is it edifying?
- Does it increase my knowledge of Him and His ways?
- Is it in harmony with the rest of Scripture?
- Does it bring a response to God of prayer, praise, thanksgiving, worship, confession or practical action?

Remember the words of the Lord Jesus: "If anyone chooses to do God's will, he will find out whether my teaching comes from God or whether I speak on my own" (John 7:17). As long as we choose to do the will of God, He will not allow us to go outside it.

What If I Am Getting Nothing from the Verse?

If you ever experience a dry period, and there seems to be no revelation, speak to the Lord about it. He loves honesty, and we can tell Him exactly how we feel and what the situation is. There are obvious questions we should ask:

- Have I obeyed what He has told me to do previously?
- Did I expect God to speak to me?
- Am I leaning on my own understanding, or am I relying on the Holy Spirit to lead me into all truth?
- Am I resisting the message of this verse in some way?

If these questions do not reveal anything wrong, rest in Him; and if nothing comes from that verse, move on to the next.

All True Meditation Will Bring a Response to God

Without apology I repeat this vital truth about meditation: It always brings a response to God. God communes with us, and we with Him.

Part of meditation is praying Scripture. That great saint who died in the eighteenth century, Madame Jeanne Guyon, whose writings greatly influenced such people as John Wesley and Jessie Penn Lewis, encouraged people to "pray the Scriptures." In praying Scripture, we do not judge by how much is read, but by

the way it is read. Madame Guyon said that reading quickly is like
a bee skimming the surface of a flower, but praying the Scripture
is like the bee penetrating deep into the depths of the flower to
remove the deepest nectar.

In the Psalms we see how David's meditation brought a variety
of responses to God.

▶ **Meditation:** "My heart grew hot within me, and as I meditated, the fire burned."
Response: Prayer—"then I spoke with my tongue" (Psalm
39:3–4).

▶ **Meditation:** "On my bed I remember you; I think of you
through the watches of the night."
Response: Praise—"Because you are my help, I sing in the
shadow of your wings" (Psalm 63:6–7).

▶ **Meditation:** "I remember the days of long ago; I meditate on
all your works and consider what your hands have done."
Response: Expressed longing for God—"I spread out my
hands to you; my soul thirsts for you like a parched land"
(Psalm 143:5–6).

We can see this too in other passages from the Psalms, such as
49:3; 77:12; 104:34; 119:48.

Can Study Be Included in Meditation?

Sometimes while meditating there is a desire to know more about
the meaning of a word or subject the verse may suggest. There is
nothing wrong with gaining more knowledge through a
concordance, commentary or dictionary. However, when you
have gained that knowledge, bring it back to the verse and
include it in your meditation.

How Can What Is Received in Meditation Be Retained?

In meditation, the Holy Spirit takes the Word and imparts it to
our hearts. That Word becomes part of us when it is received. The
Holy Spirit also brings truth to our remembrance when needed.

Jesus gave this great promise to His disciples: "But the Coun-
selor, the Holy Spirit, whom the Father will send in my name,
will teach you all things and will remind you of everything I have
said to you" (John 14:26).

Study questions:

1. How should we choose what to meditate on?
2. How do we test the thoughts that come to mind, to know whether they are from God?
3. How do we decide when to meditate, how long to go on for, and when it is best to move on to a different verse?
4. What questions can we ask when we are unable to receive during a time of meditation?
5. Have you had the experience of the Holy Spirit bringing the Word to your remembrance when you need it? Explain.

10

Beginning and Continuing
Meditation

Beginning Meditation

This is the day you can really start putting into practice the things you have been learning. Remember that meditation will be a process of learning as you do it. Are you ready?

Wait on the Lord

Be still ... Is everything all right between you and the Lord? Spend a minute or two thanking Him for His goodness and grace to you. Praise Him for who He is. Worship Him. Pour out your love to Him. Yield yourself totally to Him, trusting Him to give you His thoughts.

Open your Bible at the book God guided you to, at chapter 1. If you have not already done so, read through the first chapter so that you have a knowledge of the context. Now go to verse 1, and read the verse slowly word by word. Then reread it with an open heart and mind to receive His thoughts.

As an aid in starting, write out the first one or two verses.

_____

_____

_____

_____

_____

_____

Now write the thoughts you have received.

_____

_____

_____

_____

_____

_____

Now write what your response was to God.

_____

_____

_____

_____

_____

Summary
What did I learn about God today?

_____

_____

_____

_____

_____

What did I learn about myself?

_____

_____

_____

What did I praise Him for?

_____

_____

_____

What, and who, did I pray or intercede for?

_____

_____

_____

Is this leading me to any course of action?

_____

_____

_____

Finish by worshiping the Lord.

Choose to recall your meditation throughout the day and night, and you will find the Lord will keep giving you more, as well as establishing what you have received.

Well done for doing this. Praise the Lord!

Continuing Meditation

This is your second day. Do you remember what the Lord said to you yesterday? It has remained, has it not? Have any thoughts been added to it?

It is not necessary to write out your meditation and responses every day, unless you wish to, but the purpose of doing it again is to encourage you in the early days.

Date _____. Book _____. Chapter _____, verse _____.

Write out the verse you are meditating on today:

_____

_____

_____

_____

_____

_____

_____

_____

Your meditation:

_____

_____

_____

_____

_____

_____

Your response:

_____

_____

_____

_____

_____

_____

As you finish by praising the Lord, tell Him you are available to share with others what He has shared with you, if He opens the way for this and you sense it is His will. People like "fresh bread!"

Also, make yourself available to teach someone else to meditate. Once you have done it yourself you are qualified to lead someone else into this spiritual practice. Introduce your wife, husband, children or friends to this rewarding way of getting to know God.

Borrow David's prayer:

> May the words of my mouth and the meditation of my heart
>   be pleasing in your sight,
> O Lord, my Rock and my Redeemer.
>
> Psalm 19:14

Or use this prayer poem:

> My God, I thank you for your word
> That comes like medicine or a sword
> To change my life that I may be
> In greater likeness unto thee.
>
> Speak how you will, that is your choice,
> In thunder's peal or still, small voice.
> Your word is truth, your word is light
> To show me how to live aright.

Reveal yourself—that is my plea
Reveal yourself, O God, to me.
Show me your will, show me your ways
That I may serve you all my days.

"Let there be light," your voice did cry
And brilliant radiance filled the sky.
Command again that light to me
That I may more your glory see.

O Living Word, I praise your name.
You are forever more the same.
You spoke to prophet, priest and king,
Now speak to me, your word to bring.

I thirst for you, my God, my Lord,
And open up your sacred word.
I come to drink, I come to feed;
Please meet my very deepest need.

Come Holy Ghost, come heavenly dove.
Show me my Lord, the one I love,
And speak to me that I may say,
"Yes . . . God spoke to me today."

Give me, Lord, your revelation
Through your word in meditation.
And let it ever to me bring
The knowledge of my Lord and King.

                                        Campbell McAlpine

Study questions:

1. What verses did you meditate on?
2. How able were you to wait on the Lord?
3. What thoughts did you receive as you meditated on the words of Scripture?
4. How did you respond to God as a result of the meditation?
5. What was most valuable to you about this experience?

11

The Subjects of Meditation

As we discover in the life of David, there are several broad themes on which we can meditate. We will focus on some major subject areas as an introduction.

The Word of God

God's Word itself is a subject for meditation, as we consider its many different portrayals in Scripture. The Word is symbolized as a sword, a hammer, a scroll, fire, water, rain and seeds. The Word of God runs swiftly, feeds us, brings life, melts what is frozen, washes us, causes us to tremble, preserves us and breaks strongholds. It is right and true, flawless, living and active, and cannot be chained.

Focusing on the Word itself increases our appreciation and respect for the Scriptures. The many references to the Word of God in previous chapters can give starting points for fruitful meditation.

God the Father and His Son, Jesus Christ

There are many ways to meditate on God the Father and on the Lord Jesus. In the silence of waiting on Him, we can contemplate His greatness, ponder all the glorious facets of His perfect character and remember His faithfulness. We can reflect on His glory, grace, goodness, holiness, justice, longsuffering, love, mercy, power, wisdom, justice, judgments, knowledge and gentleness.

The result will be a response—as the hymn writer put it, we will be lost in "wonder, love and praise." Worship will rise to God for all He is, all He has done and all He has promised to do.

We can meditate on His names. We can meditate on the cross and pour out our thanksgiving for His amazing grace. We can ponder the glory and power of His resurrection, ascension and position at the right hand of God. We can contemplate His coming again.

David said:

> May my meditation be pleasing to him,
> as I rejoice in the LORD.
>
> Psalm 104:34

> My soul will be satisfied as with the richest of foods;
> with singing lips my mouth will praise you.
> On my bed I remember you;
> I think of you through the watches of the night.
>
> Psalm 63:5–6

The Work of God

> I will remember the deeds of the LORD;
> yes, I will remember your miracles of long ago.
> I will meditate on all your works
> and consider all your mighty deeds.
>
> Psalm 77:11–12

Remembering all the works God has done in the past is not only an incentive to praise, but a stimulus to faith. Many times in the Scripture the writers deliberately bring to remembrance the works of God. David cries in Psalm 105:5–6:

> Remember the wonders he has done,
> his miracles, and the judgments he pronounced,
> O descendants of Abraham his servant,
> O sons of Jacob, his chosen ones.

Many of the psalms are taken up with the mighty things God has done in history, to encourage us to trust Him for the present and the future. Just prior to his death, Moses gathered the children of Israel together. To give them courage to take possession of the Promised Land, he recounted the great things God had done in delivering them from Egypt and providing for them in the wilderness.

You, too, can remember the things God has done for you and for others in the past. As the old hymn says, "Count your many blessings, / name them one by one, / and it will surprise you / what the Lord has done." Meditate on the work of the Lord.

The Creation

The psalmist not only meditated on the work of God, but also on the works of His hands. "I remember the days of long ago; I meditate on all your works and consider what your hands have done" (Psalm 143:5).

God speaks to all of His servants, and even to unbelievers, through His creation and His creatures. Before He gave Abraham the promise of the multiplication of his seed, He told him to contemplate the works of His hands, the stars: "He took him outside and said, 'Look up at the heavens and count the stars—if indeed you can count them.' Then he said to him, 'So shall your offspring be'" (Genesis 15:5).

If we have eyes to see, there is so much that declares His greatness and causes us to worship and praise Him.

> The heavens declare the glory of God;
> the skies proclaim the work of his hands.
> Day after day they pour forth speech;
> night after night they display knowledge.
> There is no speech or language
> where their voice is not heard.
> Their voice goes out into all the earth,
> their words to the ends of the world.
>
> Psalm 19:1–4

We are asked to consider one of the smallest works of His hands, and learn from it:

> Go to the ant, you sluggard;
> consider its ways and be wise!
> It has no commander,
> no overseer or ruler,
> yet it stores its provisions in summer
> and gathers its food at harvest.
>
> Proverbs 6:6–8

Yes, God speaks in many ways and teaches many lessons, from a grain of wheat, seed that falls into the ground, trees, a rock, the grass, the lily of the field, the thunder and lightning, rain, dew, a spring of water, a mustard seed, a watered garden and so on. There is much to meditate on in His creation.

I was once teaching biblical meditation at a Bible school in Hawaii. After mentioning the practice of meditating on the works of God's hands, I took the class outside. I told them to go and sit somewhere and, in reliance on the Lord, meditate on some aspect of the natural world, allowing God to speak to them. They did so for over an hour, and then we gathered again to share what God had said.

It was staggering to hear the many insights revealed and the lessons that had been learned during that time. The God who "spoke to our forefathers through the prophets at many times and in various ways" (Hebrews 1:1) still speaks today in a great variety of ways. Meditation quickens our senses to be perceptive to what He is saying, either in the Word, while meditating on Him or His work in our lives or on the works of His creation.

May our attitude always be "Speak, Lord, for your servant is listening"—and expect an answer.

Prayer

Yes, Lord, help me to be perceptive and alert to any way or any means You choose to speak to me. Give me eyes to see and ears to hear. Amen.

Study questions:

1. What subjects are valuable themes for meditation?
2. How is remembering God's works a stimulus for faith?
3. How can the natural world speak to us of God's greatness?
4. Are there other themes or qualities of God not already listed in the text that would also be fruitful for meditation?
5. Are you perceptive and alert to the various ways in which God desires to speak to you?

12

The Final Bugle

The call to meditate is not just a suggestion of a useful technique to brighten up the "quiet time." Rather, it is a command to be disciplined, to think clearly, to be prepared, to be watchful, and above all to know God and His Son Jesus Christ. We should consider it a clear instruction from God that deserves our attention and obedience:

> Do not let this Book of the Law depart from your mouth; meditate on it day and night, so that you may be careful to do everything written in it.
>
> Joshua 1:8

> Take to heart all the words I have solemnly declared to you this day, so that you may command your children to obey carefully all the words of this law. They are not just idle words for you—they are your life. By them you will live long in the land you are crossing the Jordan to possess.
>
> Deuteronomy 32:46–47

> Give careful thought to your ways.
>
> Haggai 1:7

> Listen carefully to what I am about to tell you....
>
> Luke 9:44

We are living in days of gross darkness. The effects of evil are going to become more evident in our society. The church will be purified, and there will be a separation of the true from the false, the real from the counterfeit.

Much of Paul's writing in the epistles is directed by an awareness of the perilous situations of those to whom he wrote. As year succeeds year, it seems that our circumstances as believers place us increasingly in the context of Paul's readers. We witness earthquakes, floods, fires, nation warring against nation, increase in crime and violence, with politicians impotent to deal with such disorder.

The church has too often been seen as an institution sitting at cross-denominational discussions or as factions at cross-purposes with each other. Ironically, the impact and demands of the cross of Christ have not surfaced through the agenda.

The call to meditate is a call to heed the words of God, because only His words minister life, release life, illuminate our thinking on the greatest matters we can know—the mighty character of God and His purposes for our lives, the Church, the world and for eternity.

There is an urgent need in our day to be sharpened in the way we approach the things of God. Assurance of salvation has often led to a kind of self-centered smugness that has strangled spiritual life. In many areas of the church we are cultivating our own gardens unmindful of the havoc wreaked by the war of darkness against human souls.

To meditate is to be continually exposed to the work of the Holy Spirit, who through the Word of God will lead us from self-examination to examination of the world in which we live. As we observe with God's eyes, we will be mobilized to give our lives even as God gave His only Son. The abiding Word of God is the means of overcoming the evil one.

We must repent of our sloth in our dealings with God's Word. We are content with a "fruit salad" of religious ideas and a state of affairs in the church of the living God that would not be tolerated in a school of business. The command to meditate, coming with urgency from the heart of God, is a call to think His thoughts and to learn of Him.

We cannot succeed in a battle raging for the minds of people without the mind of God. Only as the Word of God abides in us will we survive the violent collision between the mind of Christ and worldly values—the life of Christ in us will remain unshaken.

Meditation in God's Word will leave us in no doubt of the supernatural orientation of the believer. It is no exaggeration to say that it will revolutionize our lives. This is not a humanly originated assertion, but the promise of God.

> He is like a tree planted by streams of water,
>   which yields its fruit in season
> and whose leaf does not wither.
>   Whatever he does prospers.
>
> Psalm 1:3

Meditation requires discipline and perseverance. The more we know God, the greater menace we are to the kingdom of darkness; therefore, opposition can be expected. But there is victorious power in the name of Jesus. Daniel spoke of a coming force of evil, but says, "the people who know their God will firmly resist him. Those who are wise will instruct many" (Daniel 11:32–33). The New King James Version puts it this way: "The people who know their God shall be strong, and carry out great exploits. And those of the people who understand shall instruct many."

There is no greater knowledge on earth than the knowledge of the God of heaven. The prophet Jeremiah declared this, so let him have the closing word:

This is what the LORD says:

"Let not the wise man boast of his wisdom
   or the strong man boast of his strength
   or the rich man boast of his riches,
but let him who boasts boast about this:
   that he understands and knows me,
that I am the LORD, who exercises kindness,
   justice and righteousness on earth,
   for in these I delight,"

declares the LORD.
Jeremiah 9:23–24

Study questions:

1. Explain how the call to meditate is actually a command from Scripture.
2. Why is it increasingly urgent to be "sharpened" in the way we approach the things of God?
3. In what way is abiding in the Scriptures necessary for surviving the clash between the mind of Christ and worldly values?
4. What is the greatest knowledge we can have on earth?
5. Are you committing yourself wholeheartedly to the challenge of meditating daily on God's Word?

Campbell McAlpine is a highly respected Bible teacher and speaker. He has authored a number of books, including *The Practice of Biblical Meditation* and *The Leadership of Jesus*. He also provides spiritual covering and advice to Lydia Fellowship International, a global intercessory prayer movement his wife, Shelagh, founded in 1977.